You've Got 21 Days to Change Your Life

A Faith-Based Journey From Laziness to Purpose

By
Nardos Abebe Yauney

Copyrights

Published by:

Trinity Publishing Press

Table Of Contents

About The Author

Nardos Abebe Yauney was born and raised in the small town of Nazreth, Ethiopia. From a young age, she carried a deep curiosity about life, faith, and creativity. Her early work experiences in local restaurants introduced her to the beauty of hard work, community, and resilience values that have shaped both her art and her message.

As a young adult, Nardos moved to Washington, D.C., where she embraced a new culture and language. Her journey across continents, from Africa to the United States, opened her eyes to the power of purpose, transformation, and divine timing. Along the way, she discovered that every experience—whether joyful or painful—was part of God's greater plan to refine her character and deepen her faith.

A passionate artist, wife, mother and woman of faith, Nardos expresses her creativity through painting, mosaic art, and writing. Her work reflects themes of healing, identity, and spiritual renewal, inspiring others to rediscover who they are in Christ.

Her book, *You've Got 21 Days to Change Your Life,* is a heartfelt invitation to reset the mind, heal the heart, and align one's life with God's divine purpose. Drawing from her personal journey of faith and transformation, Nardos guides readers through a 21- day path of reflection, forgiveness, gratitude, and renewed purpose.

Now based in the United States, she continues to write, create, and encourage others to rise above challenges, embrace change, and walk boldly in their God-given identity and calling.

You've Got 21 Days to Change Your Life

Introduction: From Stuck to Set Free

"The soul of the lazy man desires and has nothing. But the soul of the diligent shall be made rich."

— **Proverbs 13:4**

Have you ever felt like you were meant for more, but just couldn't get moving?

Perhaps your days blur together. You scroll more than you pray. You dream big, but you do little. You talk about change, but fall back into the same habits.

You're not alone… and you're not hopeless.

This book is for the believer who feels stuck, slow, tired, lazy, or lost. The world calls it procrastination. However, the Bible calls it slothfulness. But the truth is, it's a spiritual battle.

We are living in a time where distractions are everywhere, and comfort is worshipped. But Jesus didn't live a lazy life. He lived on assignment.

Jesus?

He rose early to pray.

"Very early in the morning, while it was still dark, Jesus got up, left the house and went off to a solitary place, where he prayed."

— **Mark 1:35**

He walked for miles to serve.

"Jesus went through all the towns and villages, teaching in their synagogues, proclaiming the good news of the kingdom and healing every disease and sickness."

— **Matthew 9:35**

He fasted for 40 days.

"After fasting forty days and forty nights, he was hungry."

— **Matthew 4:2**

Even when He rested, it was intentional.

"Then, because so many people were coming and going that they did not even have a chance to eat, he said to them, 'Come with me by yourselves to a quiet place and get some rest.'"

— **Mark 6:31**

He taught, healed, loved, wept, and lived with purpose.

Jesus is your model.

Not the influencers, the motivational speakers, or even your feelings.

Why 21 Days?

In the Bible, the number 21 represents a time of breakthrough after prayer and fasting. In Daniel 10, Daniel fasted and prayed for 21 days, and on the final day, the angel came with his answer.

This is your "Daniel moment." Your time to fast, pray, take action, and believe for a breakthrough.

What This Book Will Do:

- Help you break the habit of laziness and procrastination
- Give you a daily dose of Scripture, prayer, and reflection
- Align your habits with the lifestyle of Jesus
- Challenge your comfort zone
- Encourage fasting, meditation, and discipline
- Help you live with spiritual fire and practical purpose

What You'll Need:

- A Bible
- A journal or notebook
- A heart ready to change
- A willingness to fast and pray
- A schedule you're ready to surrender to God

As you can see, to get the most out of this book and welcome real change, you will need to take action. You will need these items to take to heart the things written here, study the scripture prompts, and honestly write your thoughts that you will use to help you take action.

This is not a self-help book, but a God-help-me move book, seeking divine help to reveal and show you how life can be lived for the purpose for which we were created. If you are here, it is no coincidence.

You do not have to wait another year to change. You've got 21 days, and a Savior who walks with you every step of the way.

Let's begin.

Day 1: Face Yourself

Theme: Confront the Real You, Without Excuses

"Search me, O God, and know my heart. Try me and know my thoughts."

— Psalm 139:23

Devotional Thought: Most people never change because they never face the truth. They hide behind distractions. They blame their past. They delay what God has called them to do. But change always begins with honesty.

Today is not about judgment. It is about awareness.

It's time to ask yourself, "Why am I really stuck? Why do I stay lazy? What am I afraid of?"

Even Adam hid when he sinned. But God came looking and asked, "Where are you?"

He wasn't asking for location; He was asking for truth.

You can't defeat what you won't face.

You can't change what you keep denying.

But once you're honest, the healing

begins. **Biblical Example: David**

David was called a man after God's heart, not because he was perfect, but because he faced his sins, his fears, and his failures. He said, "I acknowledged my sin to You, and I did not cover my iniquity..." (Psalm 32:5)

Laziness is often a cover for deeper wounds. It may be fear of failure, past trauma, or low confidence, but Jesus can heal all of that. You just need to show up.

Prayer:

"Father,

I surrender my excuses, my pride, and my laziness.

Shine Your light into every hidden part of my heart.

Help me see what's stopping me—and give me the courage to change.

Search me, test me, and show me where I've been passive or afraid.

I want to live with purpose, not shame.

I want to walk with You, not wander alone.

In Jesus' name, Amen."

Scriptures to meditate:

- Psalm 139:23-24
- Proverbs 13:4
- John 8:32
- Romans 12:2

Journal Prompt:

- Where in my life have I allowed laziness or fear to win?
- What excuses do I keep telling myself that I need to stop?
- What does the "old me" need to let go of

starting today?

Action Step: Be brutally honest with yourself.

Write down 3 areas of your life where laziness has kept you from obeying God or moving forward (e.g., health, business, prayer life, finances, and relationships).

Commit these areas to God in prayer.

Fasting Challenge:

Start small…

Fast from entertainment or social media for the next 24 hours. Use that time to pray, journal, and reflect.

You've taken your first step, not by trying to impress God, but by being real with Him. He loves the real you, and He's ready to build a new you.

Prayer + Fasting Guide

(Use this guide here and for Day 15: Fast Biblically)

Spiritual Discipline for Real Transformation

"However, this kind does not go out except by prayer and fasting."

— **Matthew 17:21**

When you are ready, step up your fasting to include abstention from food.

Why Pray and Fast?

If laziness has a grip on your life, you need more than

motivation. You need spiritual power.

Prayer aligns your heart with God.

Fasting overcomes your flesh and bodily desires and clears the noise.

Together, they open the door for a breakthrough.

Jesus fasted.

Daniel fasted.

Esther fasted.

The early church fasted.

And you can too.

Fasting is a weapon

Fasting is not a diet, and it is definitely not a punishment. It is a spiritual discipline to say, "God, I want You more than I want comfort."

It breaks chains, trains your spirit, and humbles your heart before God.

How to Fast During This 21-Day Challenge:

You can choose one or a mix throughout the 21 days:

1. **Daniel Fast**

   Fruits, vegetables, water (see Daniel 10:2–3)

   No meat, sugar, or processed foods.

2. **Partial Fast**

   Skip one or two meals a day and use that time to

pray

3. Full Fast (1–3 Days Only)

Water only, for physically and spiritually prepared individuals.

Check with a doctor if you are unsure.

4. Media Fast

Cut out social media, TV, or digital distractions.

Use that time to read your Bible and journal.

When You Fast:

- Start with prayer: Ask the Holy Spirit to guide your fast
- Set a clear goal: Healing, breakthrough, direction, discipline, etc.
- Use your extra time to pray, read Scripture, or worship
- Keep a journal: Write what you're hearing from God
- Stay humble: Don't brag or boast about your fast

"When you fast… do not be like the hypocrites…"
(Matthew 6:16-18)

Daily Prayer Schedule Idea:

- Morning: Start your day with Scripture and surrender
- Midday: Quick prayer check-in (Psalm 55:17)
- Evening: Reflect, repent, and worship

You don't need hours. Just consistency and an open heart.

What to expect spiritually:

- Greater spiritual sensitivity
- Clarity and direction
- Conviction and healing
- Stronger discipline
- Fresh hunger for the Word
- Emotional healing
- Victory over old patterns

Tips for Success

- Stay hydrated
- Plan your meals ahead (for a Daniel Fast)
- Tell a trusted prayer partner
- Don't beat yourself up if you slip, get back up
- Let grace lead, not guilt

Suggested Weekly Focus:

- Week 1: Media Fast with light food restriction
- Week 2: Daniel Fast or skip one meal daily
- Week 3: Choose 1–3 days to fully fast or add deeper prayer times

Final Word:

Fasting is not easy, but it is powerful. It is a secret weapon to break the grip of laziness and awaken your spirit. Don't fast to earn God's love, but to fight for your future.

Day 2: Define Your "Why"
Theme: Finding Your God-Given Purpose

"For I know the plans I have for you," declares the Lord, "plans to prosper you and not to harm you, plans to give you a hope and a future."

— Jeremiah 29:11

Devotional Thought: Change feels impossible without a powerful reason. But when your "why" is rooted in God's purpose for you, laziness loses its grip.

God created you with a unique calling, a mission only you can fulfill. Your "why" is the fuel that will move you when motivation runs dry.

Jesus lived with purpose every day, knowing why He came and what He had to do.

Today, it's your turn to uncover your God-given why. This isn't about what the world expects, but it's about what God designed you for.

Prayer:

"Father,

Reveal to me today the purpose You have for my life.

Show me why You created me and how You want to use me.

Help me embrace this calling with passion and courage.

Let Your plans be my plans, and Your will my will.

In Jesus' name, Amen."

Scriptures to Meditate:

- Proverbs 19:21
- Ephesians 2:10
- Romans 8:28
- Psalm 138:8

Journal Prompt:

- What do I feel passionate about?
- What gifts or talents has God given me?
- How can I use these to serve others and glorify God?
- What would my life look like if I lived fully on purpose?

Action Step:

Write a clear statement of your "Why" today.

Example: "I am called to serve others by [your gift] to bring glory to God."

Keep it somewhere you'll see it daily.

Day 3: Destroy the Lazy Mindset

Theme: Renew Your Mind, Break the Cycle

"Do not be conformed to this world, but be transformed by the renewing of your mind, so that you may prove what is the good and acceptable and perfect will of God."

— Romans 12:2

Devotional Thought: Laziness starts in the mind. Negative thoughts, excuses, and defeatist beliefs trap you in a cycle of inactivity.

But God wants your mind to be renewed—cleared of doubt, fear, and complacency—and filled with His truth.

Jesus never wasted time or energy on excuses. He knew His mission and stayed focused. You can do the same by feeding your mind with Scripture and casting out lies.

Prayer:

"Father,

Help me to reject the lies that tell me I'm too tired, too weak, or too late.

Renew my mind daily with Your truth.

Fill me with the mindset of a warrior, a doer, and a believer.

Help me focus on Your will above my feelings or fears.

Scriptures to Meditate:

- Philippians 4:13
- 2 Timothy 1:7
- Isaiah 40:31
- Colossians 3:2

Journal Prompt:

- What lies about myself do I believe keep me lazy?

- How can I replace those lies with God's truth?

- What daily habits can help me renew my mind?

Action Step:

Choose 3 powerful Scripture verses that help you combat laziness and memorize or write them on cards.

Read or say these out loud every morning and whenever you feel tempted to give in to laziness.

Day 4: Get Up and Walk
Theme: Obedience Over Comfort

"Jesus said to him, 'Get up, take up your bed, and walk.' Immediately, he was healed, and he took up his bed and walked."

— John 5:8-9

Devotional Thought: Sometimes, the biggest battle is simply rising up. Laziness whispers, "Stay still, rest more, wait longer." But God says, "Get up."

Jesus healed a man who had been inactive for 38 years simply by commanding him to rise and walk. The power was already there; all he had to do was obey.

Your breakthrough starts with obedience, no matter how small the step.

Prayer:

"Father,

Give me the strength to rise today, no matter how heavy my spirit feels.

Help me take the first step, even if the path isn't clear yet.

May my actions honor You and lead me closer to Your purpose.

In Jesus' name, Amen."

Scriptures to Meditate:

- Isaiah 40:31
- Philippians 3:14
- Hebrews 12:1

Journal Prompt:

- What is one small step I can take today toward my goals?
- What fears or doubts are holding me back?
- How can I lean on God to overcome them?

Action Step:

Pick one task you've been procrastinating on. Break it into tiny steps and commit to completing the first one today.

Day 5: Write Your Life Vision

Theme: See It. Speak It. Write It.

"Write the vision and make it plain on tablets, that he may run who reads it."

— Habakkuk 2:2

Devotional Thought: You can't live with purpose if you don't know where you're going. God gives vision not to impress you, but to direct you.

Lazy people drift. Purposeful people write. When you write your vision, you're partnering with God to shape your future.

Jesus always had a clear mission: "I came to do the will of Him who sent me."

— John 6:38

He walked, taught, healed, prayed, and suffered all because He knew the why and the where. It's time for you to clarify your vision, not just for success, but for significance in Christ.

Prayer:

"Father,

I want to live on purpose—not by accident, not by fear.

Give me vision for my life that aligns with Your will.

Help me to dream boldly, write clearly, and act faithfully.

Use my gifts for Your glory.

In Jesus' name, Amen."

Scriptures to Meditate:

- Habakkuk 2:2-3
- Jeremiah 1:5
- Proverbs 16:3
- Ephesians 2:10

Journal Prompt:

- What kind of person do I want to become over the next year?
- What areas of my life need vision: spiritual, health, finances, relationships, career, and calling?
- What legacy do I want to leave behind?

Action Step:

Take time and effort to write your life vision.

A person's life vision usually evolves over time and changes as we change and grow older. But many people simply "go with the flow" and never really define or try to find their life vision.

It's best to start small and ask, "What are the big things in life that are really important to me that I want to do or accomplish?" After prayerful consideration and careful thought, write those big things down. Take time today and start that list. Over the course of this 21-day challenge, revisit the list daily and make changes to it, but more importantly, fill in the details and action steps that you can take starting today. Think ahead and write future action steps and details that you can do after one part of your vision is already fulfilled.

After the 21-day challenge, revisit your life vision list at least once a year, such as on your birthday or at the New Year, and revise it as needed.

Be bold. Be honest. Be prayerful.

Start with:

"By God's grace, I see myself becoming a person who…"

Then break your vision into the following 3 categories to start:

1. Who I want to be (character, faith, mindset)
2. What I want to do (career, ministry, impact)
3. How I want to live (daily habits, relationships, values)

When you write your vision, you give your soul a direction, and your faith a target.

Post it where you'll see it. Speak it over yourself. Pray it daily.

Day 6: Start Your Day with God

Theme: Seek First, Move in Power

"Very early in the morning, while it was still dark, Jesus got up, left the house, and went off to a solitary place, where He prayed."

— Mark 1:35

Devotional Thought: How you start your day shapes how you live your life. Jesus, the Son of God, rose early to pray before anyone else moved. He didn't begin His day with distraction; He began with direction.

If Jesus needed quiet time with the Father… how much more do we?

Starting your day with God doesn't have to be long; instead, it just has to be intentional.

Even a 10–15-minute break can break spiritual laziness, renew your mind, and remind you of your purpose.

Prayer:

"Father,

Thank You for waking me up today.

Before I scroll, eat, or speak—I come to You.

Lead my thoughts, order my steps, and fill me with Your Spirit.

Help me seek You first and not the world.

May this day bring glory to Your name.

In Jesus' name, Amen."

Scriptures to Meditate:

- Psalm 5:3
- Matthew 6:33
- Isaiah 50:4
- Proverbs 8:17

Journal Prompt:

- What usually distracts me in the morning?
- How can I create a simple routine to connect with God first thing?
- What do I need to let go of to make space for Morning Prayer?

Action Step:

Create your Morning with God Plan.

Choose a time and place. Start with:

- 5 minutes of prayer
- 5 minutes of reading Scripture
- 5 minutes of journaling or worship

Set your alarm 15 minutes earlier tonight, and start tomorrow with God.

Laziness dies when discipline is born. And discipline is born when you seek God before the world.

Day 7: Reflect and Reset

Theme: Look Back, Give Thanks, and Adjust

"Let us examine our ways and test them, and let us return to the Lord."

— Lamentations 3:40

Devotional Thought: You've made it through your first week. That's powerful. But growth isn't just about moving forward; it's also about pausing to reflect.

This journey isn't about perfection. It's about progress.

Jesus often withdrew to reflect and pray. (Luke 5:16)

He rested, re-centered, and reset His focus before moving forward again.

Today is your day to sit with God, reflect on what He's shown you, and prepare your heart for even greater growth in Week 2.

Prayer:

"Father,

Thank You for the strength to get through this first week.

Show me where I've grown—and where I need grace.

Help me let go of any guilt, distraction, or fear.

I choose today to rest in You and prepare to rise stronger tomorrow.

In Jesus' name, Amen."

Scriptures to Meditate:

- Psalm 139:23–24
- 2 Corinthians 13:5
- Isaiah 43:18–19
- Luke 5:16

Journal Prompt:

- What have I learned about myself this week?
- How have I grown spiritually, mentally, or emotionally?
- What held me back this week, and what helped me move forward?
- What one habit will I carry into Week 2?

Action Step:

- Take 15–30 minutes today to sit quietly, pray, and journal.
- Fast or unplug for a few hours if possible.
- Review Days 1–6. Reread your vision and remind yourself: You are not who you were a week ago.

Reflection renews your

vision. Rest resets your

strength.

Now you're ready to go deeper. Week

1 Complete: Wake Up in Christ

Let's move into Week 2: Discipline is Love, where we

train our body, mind, and spirit to walk in victory and not fall back.

24

Day 8: Master Your Time

Theme: Don't Let Time Manage You—You Manage It

"Be very careful, then, how you live, not as unwise but as wise, making the most of every opportunity, because the days are evil."

– Ephesians 5:15–16

Devotional Thought: You don't "find" time—you make time. Laziness loves wasted time. But discipline loves intentional time.

Every person on Earth gets the same 24 hours. The difference? It's in how we use it.

Jesus had a short time on Earth, but He used every moment wisely through:

- Early prayer (Mark 1:35)
- Teaching and healing (Luke 4:43)
- Resting when needed (Mark 6:31)
- Spending time with His disciples (John 15:15)

Time is holy.

Time is life.

And once it's gone, you don't get it back.

Prayer:

"Father,

Forgive me for the time I've wasted.

Help me number my days and live with urgency and peace.

Teach me to prioritize what matters and release what doesn't.

Let my time serve my purpose—not my laziness.

In Jesus' name, Amen."

Scriptures to Meditate:

- Psalm 90:12
- Ecclesiastes 3:1
- Proverbs 6:10–11
- Luke 12:35–40

Journal Prompt:

- What are my top 3 time-wasters?
- What time in my day could be given back to God?
- How would Jesus use 24 hours if He were me?

Action Step:

Create a "Time Redemption Plan."

1. Pick 3 things to remove this week (examples: TV binges, social media scrolling, sleeping late).
2. Pick 3 things to add (examples: Bible reading, walking, journaling, working on a goal).
3. Choose a specific time block each day to give to God (morning, lunch, or evening).

Laziness is often disguised as "I don't have time." But when you walk with God, you'll always have time for what matters.

Day 9: Do Hard Things with Christ

Theme: No More Easy Roads. Choose the Cross

"I can do all things through Christ who strengthens me."

— Philippians 4:13

Devotional Thought: "Laziness often shows up when things feel hard. You start something and then quit when it gets uncomfortable. But God didn't call you to easy. He called you to obedience, even when it's hard."

Jesus didn't run from the cross, but He carried it.

He endured betrayal, beatings, temptation, pressure, and pain, yet still completed His mission.

You don't have to rely on your own strength. When it gets hard, Christ steps in.

Discipline. Focus. Endurance. These don't come naturally, but are built through resistance.

So today, push through something that feels hard, and let heaven strengthen you.

Prayer:

"Father,

When it's hard, remind me You are near.

When I want to quit, give me supernatural strength.

Help me push past the comfort zone and walk in obedience—step by step.

I will not fear hard things, because You are with me.

In Jesus' name, Amen.

Scriptures to Meditate:

- James 1:12
- Galatians 6:9
- Hebrews 12:2–3
- 2 Corinthians 12:9

Journal Prompt:

- What hard thing have I been avoiding out of fear or laziness?
- How would I face this differently if I believed Christ was giving me strength?
- What hard thing have I already overcome with God's help?

Action Step:

Do one hard thing today.

Ideas:

- Wake up earlier than usual
- Start that task you've been putting off
- Go for a walk instead of scrolling
- Speak the truth in love
- Pray even when you don't feel like it

Then write: "I did this hard thing with Christ's help." Spiritual growth doesn't come from doing what is easy, but from what is eternal. You were made to do hard things because you don't have to do them alone.

Day 10: No More Zero Days

Theme: Do Something Every Day, Even If It's Small

"Whatever you do, work at it with all your heart, as working for the Lord, not for human masters."

— Colossians 3:23

Devotional Thought: The enemy of progress isn't failure, it's doing nothing.

A "zero day" is when you make zero effort toward your growth, calling, or healing. And when you stack too many zero days, you stay stuck.

But here's the truth: Small steps still move you forward. Even if you only read one verse, take a walk, or say a 2-minute prayer. It counts.

Jesus said even a mustard seed of faith moves mountains. (Matthew 17:20)

He never despised small beginnings, and neither should you.

Today, let's kill the all-or-nothing mindset. Forget perfection. Just do one thing that aligns with the person God is calling you to be.

Prayer:

"Father,

Forgive me for wasting the days You gave me to grow.

I don't want to be paralyzed by perfection or fear.

Help me commit to progress—not performance.

Give me the grace to do what I can with what I have.

In Jesus' name, Amen."

Scriptures to Meditate:

- Zechariah 4:10
- Matthew 17:20
- Ecclesiastes 11:6
- Proverbs 13:4

Journal Prompt:

- What "small win" can I celebrate from yesterday or today?
- What simple action can I take right now to move forward?
- Why is showing up every day more important than being perfect?

Action Step:

No Zero Days. Starting now.

Pick one area of growth (spiritual, physical, emotional, or financial). Then take one intentional action today, even if it only takes 5 minutes.

Write this down: "Today, I chose progress over perfection. No zero days."

Your destiny is built in small, quiet moments of obedience. Show up today, even if it's messy, small, or slow.

Day 11: Stop Scrolling

Theme: Reclaim Your Mind from Distraction

"Set your minds on things above, not on earthly things."

— Colossians 3:2

Devotional Thought: Let's be honest: Scrolling feels good, but it steals more than it gives.

Social media can inspire, yes, but it can also feed unhealthy comparison, distraction, jealousy, and laziness. What starts as "a quick scroll" turns into lost hours and spiritual numbness.

Jesus didn't scroll. He withdrew. He silenced the noise. He spent time with the Father. He guarded His mind, even in the middle of crowds.

Your brain is powerful. But if you give it too much junk food, it loses focus, strength, and clarity.

Today, let's unplug and give our minds—and souls—back to God.

Prayer:

"Father,

Forgive me for giving more attention to my screen than to Your voice.

Train my eyes to see what matters.

Renew my mind and cleanse me of distraction.

Help me choose presence over pixels.

In Jesus' name, Amen."

Scriptures to Meditate:

- Romans 12:2
- Psalm 101:3
- Philippians 4:8
- Luke 5:16

Journal Prompt:

- How much time do I spend scrolling each day (honestly)?
- How does my mood change after long screen time sessions?
- What would my life look like if I used that time to build my mind, faith, or vision?

Action Step:

Digital Detox Challenge:

- Set a timer for your social media use today (max: 30 minutes).
- Choose 1–2 hours of screen-free time and use it to:
  - o Read the Bible
  - o Journal
  - o Pray or worship
  - o Walk and reflect
  - o Start a creative project

Then write: "I gave God my attention today, and I feel lighter, freer, and clearer."

Scrolling numbs. Presence heals.

You were created to create, not just consume.

Day 12: Train Your Body

Theme: Your Body Is a Temple, Not a Trash Can

"Do you not know that your bodies are temples of the Holy Spirit? Therefore, honor God with your bodies."

— 1 Corinthians 6:19–20

Devotional Thought: Your body is holy.

God didn't just save your spirit. He calls you to steward your body, too.

Laziness shows up in how we move (or don't), what we eat, how we rest, and whether we treat our body as sacred.

Jesus walked miles. He rose early. He fasted. He rested. He didn't overeat or live in excess. He lived in discipline and purpose.

Your body is a vessel of purpose, not just for looks, but for mission. When you train your body, you're saying, "I'm available for God's use. Strong, clear, and ready."

Prayer:

"Father,

Thank You for this body—even if it's not perfect.

Help me treat it like a gift, not a garbage bin.

Give me the strength to move it, the discipline to fuel it, and the grace to rest it.

Let my body glorify You, not my laziness.

In Jesus' name, Amen."

Scriptures to Meditate:

- 1 Timothy 4:8
- Romans 12:1
- Proverbs 23:2
- Psalm 127:2

Journal Prompt:

- Am I treating my body like it belongs to God?
- How have I neglected my physical health due to laziness or avoidance?
- What small, consistent action can I take this week to strengthen my body?

Action Step:

Choose ONE of the following today:

- Go for a 20+ minute walk (no phone).
- Prepare a healthy meal and pray before eating.
- Stretch or do light movement for 15 mins.
- Take a nap only if your body truly needs rest—not out of boredom.
- Skip one unhealthy habit (sugar, soda, overeating, etc.)

Then write: "Today I honored God with my body, and I feel stronger."

When your body is strong, your spirit has more room to thrive. Remember, discipline in your body leads to freedom in your mind. You are building strength across every part of your life—body, mind, spirit, and soul.

Day 13: Conquer the Morning
Theme: Wake Up with Heaven Just as Jesus Did

"Very early in the morning, while it was still dark, Jesus got up, left the house, and went off to a solitary place, where He prayed."

— Mark 1:35

Devotional Thought: Jesus didn't scroll. He didn't snooze. He didn't rush into chaos.

He started His day in stillness and prayer—before the world could speak, He let the Father speak first.

You don't need a "perfect" morning routine. What you need is a kingdom morning routine. One that awakens your spirit, not just your schedule.

"...great is your faithfulness." (Lamentations 3:23).

So today, don't waste it. Meet God before the world meets you.

Prayer:

"Father,

Thank You for the gift of a new day.

Let me wake with purpose, not

panic.

Give me grace to seek You first—before my phone, my to-do list, or the world.

Train me to rise in power, like Jesus.

In Jesus' name, Amen."

Scriptures to Meditate:

- Psalm 5:3
- Proverbs 8:17
- Psalm 143:8
- Isaiah 50:4

Journal Prompt:

- What is the first thing I usually do when I wake up?
- How could my life change if I consistently gave my mornings to God first?
- What distractions keep me from seeking God early?

Action Step:

Build a Morning Routine (like Jesus):

Start tomorrow with this 3-step plan:

1. Wake Up 30 Minutes Earlier
2. Pray (or journal your prayers)
3. Read 1 chapter of the Gospels

Optional Add-ons:

- Light movement/stretching
- Worship playlist
- Speak declarations over your day
- Drink water, not coffee, first

Then write: "Today, I started with heaven, and I feel

aligned, alive, and awakened."

Your mornings don't belong to laziness, dread, or your phone. They belong to the King. Start with Him, and then go on and conquer the day.

Day 14: Find Your People

Theme: You Can't Grow Alone. God Uses People

"As iron sharpens iron, so one person sharpens another."

— Proverbs 27:17

Devotional Thought: If you want to go fast, go alone. But if you want to go far, go with God-ordained people.

Jesus had a tribe. He didn't isolate, but He invited.

He surrounded Himself with people who challenged, sharpened, supported, and walked with Him. Laziness, isolation, and spiritual dryness thrive in loneliness.

You don't need a crowd. You need a circle that pushes you toward your purpose.

You are not meant to fight, grow, or rise alone. Your elevation is connected to your community.

Prayer:

"Father,

Help me find people who sharpen me—who love You more than comfort.

Show me who I need to walk with and who I need to walk away from.

Surround me with truth-speakers, faith-walkers, and vision-builders.

Let my relationships glorify You.

In Jesus' name, Amen."

Scriptures to Meditate:

- Ecclesiastes 4:9–10
- 1 Corinthians 15:33
- Hebrews 10:24–25
- Luke 6:12–13

Journal Prompt:

- Who in my life encourages my growth and faith?
- Who drains me or pulls me into laziness or negativity?
- What kind of friend or community member do I want to become?

Action Step:

Today's challenge:

- Reach out to one godly person (or someone you admire in faith).
- Ask a deep question, pray together, or plan to meet.
- OR: Attend a local Bible study, small group, or church this week.

Write this declaration:

"God is connecting me to the right people for my purpose."

The wrong people delay destiny; the right ones, however, multiply it.

Let God choose your circle, and be bold enough to walk with them.

Day 15: Fast Biblically

Theme: Align Your Body and Spirit through Fasting

"But when you fast, put oil on your head and wash your face, so that it will not be obvious to others that you are fasting, but only to your Father, who is unseen; and your Father, who sees what is done in secret, will reward you."

— Matthew 6:17-18

Devotional Thought: Fasting isn't about starving or showing off. It's about humbling yourself and opening space for God to move.

Jesus fasted for 40 days in the wilderness, strengthened by the Spirit to face temptation and carry out His mission. Fasting helps break the grip of laziness, sharpens your focus, and deepens your prayer life.

When you fast, you say, "God, I trust You more than my comfort."

Prayer:

"Father,

Teach me how to fast with humility and faith.

Help me rely on You more than food or comfort.

Use this fast to draw me closer, strengthen my spirit, and break chains of laziness.

In Jesus' name, Amen."

Scriptures to Meditate:

- Isaiah 58:6-9
- Joel 2:12-13
- Luke 4:1-2
- Acts 13:2-3

Journal Prompt:

- What is my reason or goal for fasting?
- How do I want this fast to draw me closer to God?
- What challenges might come, and how will I rely on God to overcome?

Action Step:

Plan your fast (See Prayer and Fasting Guide under Day 1 above):

1. Choose your fast type (Daniel, partial, full, media).
2. Set your start and end times.
3. Prepare your heart with prayer and a simple plan.
4. Inform a trusted prayer partner if possible.
5. Journal daily what God reveals.

Fasting is a sacred discipline reset for body, mind, spirit, and soul.

When you fast, God shows up in mighty ways.

Day 16: Break Your Excuses

Theme: Silence the Lies, and Embrace God's Truth

"Therefore, if anyone is in Christ, the new creation has come: The old has gone, the new is here!"

— 2 Corinthians 5:17

Devotional Thought: Excuses are the chains that bind laziness. They whisper lies like:

- "I'm too tired."
- "I'll start tomorrow."
- "I'm not strong enough."
- "This isn't for me."

But God's Word says you are a new creation and you are not who you were yesterday. Jesus didn't accept excuses. He pressed on, even when weary and tested.

You can too.

It's time to break free from your excuses and step into your God-given destiny.

Prayer:

"Father,

I confess the excuses I've made that have held me back.

Replace my doubts with faith, my fear with courage, my weakness with Your strength.

Help me embrace the new creation I am in Christ.

No more delays. No more excuses.

In Jesus' name, Amen."

Scriptures to Meditate:

- Romans 8:1
- Philippians 4:13
- Isaiah 41:10
- Joshua 1:9

Journal Prompt:

- What excuses have I told myself most often?
- How do these excuses keep me stuck?
- What truth from God's Word can replace these lies?
- What's one step I will take today to break free?

Action Step:

Name your top 3 excuses.

For each one, write a scripture-based response that crushes that lie.

Example:

Excuse: "I'm too weak."

Response: "I can do all things through Christ who strengthens me." — Philippians 4:13

Then declare out loud: "I am no longer a slave to excuses. I am free in Christ."

Your excuses are lies that feel comfortable, but your destiny is uncomfortable until you grow. Choose growth today.

Day 17: Build Your Prayer Life

Theme: Speak to God as if we came from Him, like He is our Father (by whom we cry out, "Abba, Father." — Romans 8:15)

"Pray without ceasing."

— 1 Thessalonians 5:17

Devotional Thought: Prayer isn't just a task on your to-do list, but a lifeline.

Jesus prayed constantly… before decisions, after miracles, even amid storms. His prayer life was intimate, honest, and powerful.

When laziness tempts you to quit or delay, prayer connects you back to your source of strength. Prayer aligns your heart with God's will, renews your mind, and activates your faith.

Prayer:

"Father,

Teach me to pray continually, with sincerity and faith.

Help me to seek You first in all things.

Make my prayer life strong, consistent, and life-giving.

In Jesus' name, Amen."

Scriptures to Meditate:

- Luke 5:16
- Philippians 4:6
- Matthew 26:41
- James 5:16

Journal Prompt:

- What does my current prayer life look like?
- When do I feel closest to God?
- How can I make prayer a natural, constant habit?
- What prayers do I want to commit to this week?

Action Step:

Set a Prayer Rhythm:

- Pick 3 daily "anchor" times to pray (morning, noon, night).
- Use simple prompts:
  o Praise
  o Confession
  o Thanksgiving
  o Supplication
  o Keep a prayer journal for answered prayers and insights.

Write: "Today, I commit to growing my prayer life, walking and talking with God every day."

Prayer is your spiritual fuel, so keep your tank full and watch your life transform.

Day 18: Meditate Like Jesus

Theme: Quiet Your Soul, Focus Your Spirit

"God is spirit, and his worshipers must worship in the Spirit and in truth."

— John 4:24

Devotional Thought: Meditation isn't just for calm, but also for connection.

Jesus knew the power of retreating into quiet places to hear the Father's voice clearly. In a noisy, busy world, meditation helps you renew your mind, focus on God's promises, and resist the enemy's lies.

Biblical meditation means thinking deeply on God's Word, letting it sink into your heart and change your thoughts.

Prayer:

"Father,

Teach me to meditate on Your Word day and night.

Help me find quiet places and moments to focus on You.

Let Your truth wash over me and transform my mind.

In Jesus' name, Amen."

Scriptures to Meditate On:

- Psalm 1:2
- Joshua 1:8
- Philippians 4:8
- Psalm 46:10

Journal Prompt:

- What Bible verses bring me peace or challenge me?
- How can I create space daily to meditate?
- What distractions steal my quiet time?
- What changes when I meditate consistently?

Action Step:

Start a Meditation Practice:

- Choose one Scripture verse or passage today.
- Find a quiet place, sit comfortably, and read it slowly 3-5 times.
- Close your eyes and repeat it softly or in your mind.
- Reflect on what God might be saying to you through it.
- Journal any insights or prayers.

Meditation connects your heart and mind to God's voice, building strength to live out His will.

Day 19: Rest Like Jesus

Theme: Sabbath Rest for Body, Mind, and Soul

"Then, because so many people were coming and going that they did not even have a chance to eat, He said to them, 'Come with Me by yourselves to a quiet place and get some rest.'"

— Mark 6:31

Devotional Thought: Rest isn't a luxury, it's a command.

Jesus modeled rest: withdrawing from crowds, sleeping in storms, and honoring the Sabbath. Rest renews your body, refreshes your mind, and restores your soul.

Without it, laziness can creep in disguised as exhaustion or burnout.

God wants you to work hard, and rest well.

Prayer:

"Father,

Help me embrace rest without guilt.

Teach me to listen when my body and soul say, "Enough."

Restore my strength so I can serve You better.

In Jesus' name, Amen."

Scriptures to Meditate:

- Exodus 20:8-11
- Matthew 11:28-30
- Psalm 23:2-3
- Hebrews 4:9-10

Journal Prompt:

- How do I currently rest? Is it intentional or accidental?
- What guilt or resistance do I feel about resting?
- How can I create a Sabbath rhythm in my week?
- When do I feel most refreshed spiritually and physically?

Action Step:

Create a Sabbath Rest Plan:

- Pick one day or half-day to unplug fully.
- Plan restful activities: prayer, reading, nature walks, naps, family time.
- Say no to work, chores, and screens as much as possible.
- Reflect and thank God for His provision and peace.

Write: "Today, I rest in God's presence and power."

Rest is fuel for faith and fruitfulness. When you rest like Jesus, you live renewed.

Day 20: Speak Life Over Yourself

Theme: Your Words Are Seeds. Plant Faith, Not Fear

"Death and life are in the power of the tongue, and those who love it will eat its fruits."

— Proverbs 18:21

Devotional Thought: Laziness often starts with negative self-talk:

- "I can't."
- "I'm too tired."
- "I'll never change."

But God's Word calls us to speak life, not death, over ourselves. Jesus declared truth over every situation: healing, hope, and purpose.

Your tongue can either plant seeds of faith that grow into victory or seeds of doubt that grow into defeat. Choose to speak about life, even when your feelings don't agree.

Prayer:

"Father,

Help me tame my tongue and speak words that build me up.

Replace my fears and doubts with Your truth and promises.

Let my words be life-giving, faith-filled, and empowering.

In Jesus' name, Amen."

Scriptures to Meditate:

- Proverbs 15:4
- James 3:5-10
- Psalm 34:1
- Joshua 1:8

Journal Prompt:

- What negative things have I said about myself?
- How can I replace them with God's truth?
- What positive affirmations will I declare daily?
- How do my words affect my motivation and actions?

Action Step:

Create your life-affirming declarations:

Write down 5 positive, faith-filled declarations from Scripture or inspired by God's promises.

Examples:

- "I am strong in Christ."
- "I can do all things through Him."
- "God has a purpose for my life."
- "I go above and beyond."
- "I am a winner."

Speak these aloud every morning and night: "I speak life over my body, mind, and spirit."

Your words create your world. Speak faith, hope, and
power daily.

Day 21: Live the Change

Theme: Your New Life Is Now, Live It Out Boldly

"Therefore, if anyone is in Christ, the new creation has come: The old has gone, the new is here!"

— 2 Corinthians 5:17

Devotional Thought: You've invested 21 days renewing your mind, disciplining your body, and walking closer with God. Now it's time to live the change daily.

Change isn't a one-time event, but a lifestyle. Jesus didn't just teach transformation, He embodied it… day after day.

You are no longer the person who started this journey. You are stronger, wiser, more disciplined, and deeply connected to the Father. Walk boldly in your new identity and share your story to help others.

Keep growing.

Prayer:

"Father,

Thank You for the work You've done in me these 21 days.

Help me live out this change with courage and faith.

Make me a light in my family, community, and world.

Use me to bring hope, healing, and transformation.

In Jesus' name, Amen."

Scriptures to Meditate:

- Romans 12:2
- Galatians 2:20
- Ephesians 4:22-24
- Philippians 1:6

Journal Prompt:

- What is the biggest change I've seen in myself?
- How will I maintain these habits long-term?
- Who can I encourage with my story?
- What's my next growth goal?

Action Step:

- Write a commitment statement declaring your new identity and goals.
- Share your breakthrough with a trusted friend or mentor.
- Plan a weekly review to reflect on and adjust your journey.
- Pray daily, rest well, speak life, and keep moving forward.

Write: "I am a new creation. I live in freedom, purpose, and power."

Your transformation is a gift and a responsibility. Live it fully. Walk it boldly. Inspire others with your journey.

Afterword

This book is the outcome of my own decision to change, and it draws from my own experiences, various books, the Bible, podcasts, and the practices I have undertaken to improve and enrich my own life.

While not always pleasant and sometimes uncomfortable (or even downright painful), I have deeply enjoyed and benefited from the learning process and the changes I've implemented in my own life. Through prayer, study, and other practices outlined in the book, I have been refreshed and strengthened.

But it is a continuing journey, not a one-and-done task to finish and forget about. Day 21 challenges the reader to "Live the Change." It requires discipline, structure, and effort from the reader. In this spirit, I encourage the reader to start and continue their own journey to change their life.

The End